Pensées

Reflections on Life, Politics, & Artificial Intelligence

Paul Abrahams

Published by Wheatmark®
2030 East Speedway Boulevard, Suite 106
Tucson, Arizona 85719 USA
www.wheatmark.com

ISBN: 979-8-88747-253-9
LCCN: 2024925886

Dedicated to My Beloved Grandchildren

Nitzan, Adva, and Ziv

Contents

III
ARTIFICIAL INTELLIGENCE

IV
A SIGNATURE PIECE

Author's Note

Blaise Pascal was a seventeenth-century philosopher and mathematician, one of the key figures of the Enlightenment. *Pensées* (Thoughts) was one of his major works.

Preface

Over the years, I regularly received letters around Christmastime from my friends describing their travels. For a long time I felt at a loss as to how to respond, since I hadn't been doing much traveling myself. Then the idea came to me of sharing my intellectual travels in the form of an annual essay, sent to my friends at the end of each year along with a greeting card. Eventually I had the idea of collecting these essays and disseminating them to a wider audience. Publishing them on Substack offered me a way to do that.

At 89 I'm wiser than I was in my teens, but not nearly as clever. Much of the wisdom I've acquired lies in learning how many implausible things are true. I hope this viewpoint will emerge through some of the less common ideas in these essays.

I've also wondered what sort of things I as a grandfather can say to my three grandchildren that they will be able to grasp without thinking that this is just an old man talking. I hope that this collection will in time serve as a legacy of useful ideas for them to ponder.

I want to express my deep gratitude to my beloved sister Nan Rubin, who made this possible by collecting the essays, organizing the collection, and publishing it in book form.

I
Reflections on Life

The Tolerant Atheist

I am an atheist; but atheism, like any other belief pertaining to deities, is based on faith—in this case, the belief that there is no God. Neither the existence nor the nonexistence of God is provable. We each believe what we believe because it explains the world to us better than any other set of beliefs.

Both atheists and theists try to argue their case on the basis of how the universe came into being. For a theist, there has to be a Creator—the notion of a world that came into existence of its own accord is simply inconceivable. For an atheist, on the other hand, the existence of a Creator seems to imply an impossible infinite regress; who or what created the Creator, and how was the Creator's Creator created? Physicists now generally agree on the Big Bang theory, which proposes that the universe arose from a single super-dense concentration of energy that then expanded, but the Big Bang theory is consistent both with the existence of a Creator and the nonexistence of a Creator.

In fact, the human mind is incapable of visualizing any origin of the universe at all. The first verse of the Bible states that "In the beginning, God created the heavens and the earth." Yet we cannot conceive of a time that has no previous time, which is what the "beginning" must be. The Big Bang has the same problem: what came before it? How can the creation of time be part of the Big Bang, as cosmologists assume, if the very notion of creation implies a time prior to the creation?

"Inconceivable" and "impossible" are not the same thing. Our minds are limited; there are things we cannot conceive that are nonetheless possible. It has to be that way because nothing else can explain the paradox of a time when there was no time. We (cosmologists, anyway) can analyze these inconceivable things using the tools of mathematics, but being able to analyze them does not imply being able to form mental images of them.

Atheism has gotten a lot of attention thanks in large part to three books: "The God Delusion" by Richard Dawkins, "The End of Faith" by Sam Harris, and "God is Not Great" by Christopher Hitchens. So far I've read only Dawkins's book. Dawkins isn't just an atheist; he's an aggressive atheist who regards theistic beliefs as ridiculous. Yet he alludes to the fact that some of his best friends are members of the godly community.

We atheists must face the fact that there are many theists, and even believers in "intelligent design", who are neither stupid nor crazy. (The theists owe the atheists the same respect, of course.) So how can intelligent, sane people reach such different conclusions about God? The answer, of course, is that they have faith in different worldviews, and such faith is capable neither of proof nor refutation.

I firmly believe that there is no god, or at least no god who makes any difference (more about that later). I could argue that science backs me up in that belief, and the cosmology of the Big Bang seems almost irrefutable. Yet I haven't examined that cosmology down to its finest details, and few others except for professionals have or are even able to. I base my understanding of it on what I am told by physicists and astronomers, whom I find more believable than soothsayers and preachers of the Gospel. I believe the results of the physicists' experiments, but I cannot verify them for myself. The believers in salvation through faith in Jesus Christ have one advantage over atheists: they get their knowledge firsthand, through personal revelation. But we atheists have an advantage of our own:

we're better at predicting the future, and that ability makes modern technology possible.

Believers in science make much of the fact that their beliefs are based on actual observation. But observation is a less reliable guide to truth than it first appears. According to the New Testament, Jesus was a guest at a wedding where the wine ran out. He had six pots of water brought to him and turned the water into wine. A miracle, no?

Now imagine the same scenario of six pots of water being turned into six pots of wine, but change the context: a professional magician performs the same "miracle" for a theater audience. Neither the magician nor the audience thinks that God or Jesus has anything to do with it, even though the audience cannot explain how it happened. A miracle in one context is a clever magic trick in another.

Science does have an advantage in this matter: experiments are repeatable but miracles are not. Following the Sermon on the Mount, Jesus healed a leper, but he didn't heal another leper every week. If he had, that would have been a better demonstration of his miraculous powers — or a demonstration of what a skillful magician he was. Science experiments do have a special claim to truth: they are repeatable by others using methods that are openly described.

Most of the American Founding Fathers — Jefferson, Madison, and those thinkers — were deists, who believed in God (usually referred to as the Almighty) but regarded him as the Divine Watchmaker who set the world in motion but then left it to run by itself. They were quite down on atheists, a view that I've never been able to understand. To me, the existence or non-existence of God is ultimately an unimportant, uninteresting, and unanswerable question. The interesting question is how one's understanding of God (or non-god) affects the way one leads one's life. What does one do differently if the Divine Watchmaker exists, versus what one does if there's no god at all? Those who believe in personal salvation through Jesus Christ certainly lead their lives differently than atheists and deists; they devote considerable energy to Jesus-related activities while atheists and deists devote none at all. Interestingly, the Founding Fathers hardly ever mentioned Jesus in their writings even though they often referred to the Almighty.

Many scientists, of course, are religious. But science is not consistent with the miraculous or even with a God who answers prayers. Repeatable experiments would not be possible if God might rejigger the results. I often wonder how those religious scientists resolve that conflict of principles.

Imperfect as my knowledge of these matters may be, I still act on the basis of it because my intuition tells me that I'm right. Since certainty is not possible, I really have no other choice.

Why Are We Here?

The story is told of a preacher who was invited to preach to the patients at a mental hospital. They gathered round to hear what the preacher had to say. He began by asking the rhetorical question "Why are we here?" Immediately one of the patients piped up. "We're all here because we're not all there!"

But why are we here? The very question assumes part of the answer: we're here because our being here serves some purpose.

Yet there's no self-evident reason why our lives should have a purpose, or at least an externally given purpose. For some religious people, our purpose on earth is to glorify the Lord. But that doesn't make much sense to me; if the Lord is omnipotent, why should He need or even care about whatever glorification we humans can provide to Him? A related answer is that our purpose is to fulfill the Lord's plans for the world. But that answer, too, flounders on the issue of the Lord's omnipotence. The only explanation of the Lord's purposes that I can see is that He is playing a form of divine solitaire; He makes the rules and then commits Himself to abide by them.

God and Satan agreed to play golf. God went first and shanked his ball far to the right. But an eagle swooped down, seized the ball, and dropped it far down the fairway. No sooner had it stopped rolling when a bolt of lightning struck the fairway, creating a mound that caused the ball to roll onto the green. A swarm of ants appeared and pushed the ball into the hole—a hole in one for God! Satan looked at God with disgust and asked, "Look, God, do you want to screw around or do you want to play golf?"

To seek an answer to the question of why we are here, it helps to pose the question more broadly: why is anything here? Do people serve a different purpose than is served by cats, volcanoes, poison ivy, or the sun? My answer to that is no—everything in the universe ultimately serves the same purpose, or no purpose. We're here because we're here. But we can create purposes for ourselves, purposes that continually evolve and define our goals.

It's often been pointed out that life is a journey, not a destination. There are exceptions such as suicide bombers, but not many. If my goal in life is to amass a billion dollars, then once I've gotten that billion dollars my goal is fulfilled and I need a new goal. If my goal each day is just to get through the day, then I always have a goal, but not a very satisfying one. For a goal to be truly satisfying, it must be one that I can pursue for a lifetime but never fully reach.

Franklin Roosevelt created the March of Dimes to seek a cure for polio and secondarily to provide help for polio victims. When the Salk vaccine was discovered, the organization's primary purpose was no longer meaningful, so it pursued a different objective: the prevention of birth defects and infant mortality. When an alpinist sets the goal of climbing the highest peak on each continent, that goal needs to be reformulated when those peaks are actually summited. For instance, the new goal might be to climb all the peaks within a single year. In any event, these goals are not dictated by nature; they are created by the individual.

My life may not have a purpose, but I surely have goals, both immediate and long term. Goals exist in a hierarchy; longer-term goals imply the shorter-term goals that lead to them. Some goals are biological imperatives; hunger drives us to seek food and weariness drives us to sleep. As conscious creatures we have the opportunity to deliberately choose our longer-term goals, though most people, I would guess, don't avail themselves of that opportunity. In having long-term goals we differ from even the most intelligent of animals. It seems doubtful that elephants, for instance, have long-term goals beyond survival and propagation of the species.

Most people are propelled through life by the fear of death, or more precisely, the fear of dying. But I have come to see that differently. I had a near-death experience about a year ago, when a stomach ulcer I was quite unaware of started to bleed and I passed out. When I came to, groggy, the EMTs were tending to me. Without their help I would have bled to death without regaining consciousness. What I remember most vividly was how peaceful I felt, not anxious or distressed at all. It showed me that dying is not something I need to be afraid of, at least if it is peaceful and painless.

But my view on that might be influenced by my age. The younger we are, the more things we miss out on by dying too soon. I sometimes think of life as a meal where we look forward to each course. Once we've had dessert, there are no more courses.

Eternal life is not the blessing that it would at first seem to be. I would not want to live for ten thousand years even if I could remain in the best of health, retain my peak capacities, and satisfy all my material desires. Eventually I would run out of unfulfilled goals and my life would become excruciatingly boring.

A man went to a theatrical agent and offered him a deal. "I'll stand on the stage and in full view of the audience shoot myself in the head and die on the spot. All I ask in return is that my widow receive $10,000 from the box office receipts." The agent answered, "That's a great idea!! But what will you do for an encore?"

How We Know What We Know

Realizing how we know what we know makes us aware of the limits of our knowledge. If we think we understand the world better than we really do, we are bound to experience many disappointments and unpleasant surprises.

The solipsist believes that everything in the world is an illusion—that what we think we see has no necessary relation to reality. It's a logically unassailable position but an impossible one to maintain for any length of time. The impact of our sensory inputs is too great just to be pushed aside.

The most obvious way we know something is by observation through our five senses. Observations may be direct (I see it's raining and I hear thunder) or indirect (my battery tester tells me that this battery is dead). But what we observe is not always what is actually happening. Professional magicians, for instance, are experts in creating illusions. Eyewitness testimony in court is often later proved to be mistaken. Measuring instruments can malfunction and give incorrect readings.

Another way we know things is through memory—the storage of knowledge. Memory tells us about the past, but our memories are sometimes mistaken.

We can know things—or think we know them—through intuition. Intuition accounts for our knowing things without knowing how we know them. Intuition by its nature cannot be shared; what

I know intuitively can only be justified to other people by resorting to some other form of knowledge.

Closely related to intuition is divine inspiration. For those who experience it, this sort of knowledge is intense and beyond question. But divine inspiration, like intuition, is not directly communicable. It can, however, be contagious, as it often is in prayer meetings.

We can know things through reasoning and logic, but reasoning and logic are vulnerable to errors. We often cite "2+2=4" as an example of something that's obviously true, but how about 3975 x 6231=24,768,225? It's true but it's not obviously true; you need to verify it with a calculator or with a long and error-prone hand calculation. Interestingly, there are mathematical statements that are undecidable—that is, they can neither be proven true nor false. (That is the essence of the Godel Incompleteness Theorem.)

Perhaps the most interesting source of knowledge is testimony—what other people tell us. We are deluged by testimony—reports, stories, advertisements, gossip, news, advice, educational materials, and much else. Even our scientific knowledge is based on the testimony of scientists, most of which the average person has no way of verifying directly.

How can we know what testimony to believe? Often we can't, particularly when it comes to people who are trying to sell us something. Advertisements are a pervasive source of testimony, carefully designed to be as convincing and believable as possible. A few of them are truthful; far more are exaggerations or deceptions.

Gauging the reliability of testimony can be very difficult. Someone can make a convincing case for a hypothesis and still be wrong. When the subject is something you don't already know much about, it's not easy to spot the flaws in the argument. But several things can help in knowing what to believe: considering the source, looking for internal inconsistencies, and hearing the other side of the argument.

An instructive example is the ongoing dispute over evolution and the biblical account of creation. Within the scientific community there is almost total consensus that evolution accounts for how humans came to be and that the biblical account of creation is a myth.

Yet there are people with impressive academic credentials who defend the biblical account, people who clearly are neither unintelligent nor uninformed. Their extensive knowledge can make it very difficult for those who haven't studied the matter to see what is wrong with their arguments.

What the creationists obviously are, however, is hopelessly biased; they start with unquestioned assumptions based on their religious faith, usually fundamentalist Christianity, and shoehorn the facts into those assumptions. Knowing that bias should make you immediately suspicious of their case. Another consideration is the implausible chronology of the creation according to Genesis, which places the creation of the earth before the creation of the sun. Believing that would require denying just about all of astronomy.

As another example, consider the Kennedy assassination. No one seems to doubt that Kennedy was indeed assassinated at Dealey Plaza in Dallas on November 23, 1963, but many people question the conclusion of the Warren Commission that Kennedy was killed by a single bullet fired by Lee Harvey Oswald. Quite a few of them marshall an impressive array of evidence involving ballistics, photographs, and documents to support their explanations.

But there are many conspiracy theories and they can't all be right. A non-expert has no way of evaluating any of the arguments with confidence; you ultimately have to rely on your own judgment of whom to believe, taking into consideration what you know of the reliability of the testifiers, their biases, and the apparent consistency and completeness of their claims. For me the composition of the Warren Commission is a strong argument for the correctness of its main conclusions, even if the commission may have gotten some of the details wrong.

So confidence in what we know should be contingent and relative. Yet we have to assume that what we know with certainty is indeed true; life without that assumption would be unmanageable.

Ultimately, the only sure knowledge we have is that of our emotions and feelings. What I perceive in the world may be an illusion, but the fact that I'm perceiving it is not an illusion and cannot be denied. If I'm feeling excited, or happy, or sad, or in pain, there's no denying that that is what I'm feeling. If I lose a limb, my sense of a phantom limb is undeniable even if the limb itself is not there. No other knowledge can be as certain and correct as that.

The New American Civil War

The new American civil war is being fought on a smaller scale, but that does not make it any less bitter.

The American Civil War of 1861 was fought between the Northern states of the Union and the Southern states of the Confederacy. We now have a civil war going on where the combatants are not separated geographically. Roughly speaking, the new civil war pits urban regions against rural ones, conservatives against liberals. Congress reflects this split, of course, but the division is more fine-grained than the boundaries of congressional districts.

The American political system, with its rigid geographical boundaries, is poorly equipped to cope with the new divisions. Beyond the obvious allegiances, there is a divide between those who feel entitled to impose their rules on society and those who don't. The far-left shares with the far right an eagerness to dictate behavior; speech codes are an example of rules that many Progressives seek to impose. The differences range over a number of issues: racial disparities, wealth disparities, sexual mores, gun regulation, and even, in the case of vaccination, public health. The recent reversal of Roe v. Wade by the Supreme Court has sharpened the divide. As red states make their anti-abortion laws even stricter and more invasive, blue states not only advertise their support for abortion rights but openly advertise the protections they will provide to women who might travel to them in order to obtain abortions. We may very well see states like Texas attempt to prevent interstate travel for pregnant women, though they are unlikely to succeed at it.

The United States of America has become the Disunited States of America, and that is a big problem in and of itself. The search for a solution must begin with the recognition by all parties, from the MAGA Patriots to the Progressives, that the other side is not going to fade into insignificance. We are all stuck in the same country.

This is not a unique historical quandary. It was faced by the two major branches of Christianity, Eastern and Western; by the Catholics and Protestants of England, and also of Ireland; by the Muslims and Hindus of India; and by the Jews and Palestinians of Israel. There must be lessons to be learned from the history of these conflicts and how they were adapted to. But what are those lessons?

The first lesson is that geographic separation helps. It does not solve the problem completely because it can leave behind enclaves of populations bitterly opposed to the majority. When the majority considers itself divinely inspired, the problem becomes much worse. We see that today in the objections of many Israelis to creating a Palestinian state on the west Bank. We see it in the red state/blue state division in the USA.

The second lesson is that the emotional intensity of the conflict sometimes fades with time. Great Britain is formally a monarchy in which the monarch is the head of the Anglican Church, but Britons of different persuasions pay that fact little heed. There is no longer any major tension between Protestant and Roman Catholics in England, and those of other persuasions be they Jews, Sikhs, Muslims, or Buddhists, comfortably fit in.

Here in the USA, anti-Catholic prejudices are largely muted. Antisemitism, though it still exists ("Jews will not replace us" at Charlottesville) is also largely muted and not considered socially acceptable. Even prejudice against Blacks is slowly fading, and in a couple more generations it probably will be imperceptible. The Christian right depends on an aging cohort; it too will die out.

Sooner or later, a new generation will take over. The Supreme Court will have a completely different membership in forty years. The political complexion of the United States in 2063 is bound to be radically different from the political complexion in 2023. The unresolvable conflicts we face now will be resolved by time.

A Critical View of Democracy

Democracy is much praised but little examined. It is a poorly defined concept that is unhelpful in solving the problems of society. The American form of it does not work well.

Like most Americans, I was brought up with the idea that democracy is the best of all political systems. Winston Churchill famously said that "Democracy is the worst form of government except all the others that have been tried." But I no longer accept that sentiment unquestioningly.

What is democracy? The simplistic answer is that it is a political system in which the majority rules, but that definition leaves many unanswered questions. The American form of democracy is an atypical example; parliamentary democracy is far more common.

The American Constitution is riddled with anachronisms, starting with the Electoral College. It was never the body of wise men that the authors of the Constitution intended it to be. There is no good reason why a state's electoral votes cannot be allocated directly to the winning candidate in that state without the intervention of a body of electors—some of whom occasionally decide to vote for someone other than the candidate they are pledged to. The 2016 election showed that having the Electoral College choose the President doesn't even satisfy the principle of majority rule; Donald Trump won the Electoral College but lost the popular vote by a significant margin. 2016 is hardly the only time that happened.

The American version of democracy is particularly inept, surviving only because there is neither the will nor the mechanism to replace it. It has devolved into an incoherent battle among special interest groups ranging across the political spectrum, from the Sierra Club to the American Beverage Association, each pushing its narrow agenda through a combination of campaign funding, lobbying, and courtroom interventions. I support and sympathize with some of these groups, but they are special interests nonetheless.

The United States of America is, as the name implies, a union of individual states, with each state treated as a political unit. Senators, for example, are chosen by the voters of each state to represent that state and only that state. Aside from its other problems, this structure assumes that a state is a community bound together by common interests—which it rarely is.

Multi-candidate races are problematic. Ranked-choice voting, which is now used in Alaska among other places, helps with this problem. It is a great improvement over plurality voting, in which the candidate with the most votes wins, but it isn't perfect. In fact, no voting protocol can be perfect; this fact was demonstrated in 1951 by the economist Kenneth Arrow, a result known as Arrow's Impossibility Theorem.

Parliamentary democracy sometimes does better, but not by much. The Israeli Knesset is a sad example of parliamentary democracy run amok, where the Orthodox parties, being essential to the majority needed to form a government, pretty much get to dictate their narrow agenda even though most of the country opposes it.

Democracy has worked well in the Scandinavian countries, but they have prospering economies and a fairly homogeneous population. Immigration to those countries has lately placed their political systems under increasing stress. The Scandinavians are torn between sympathy for the immigrants and difficulty with the economic and social stresses that immigration has created.

Representative democracy has fundamental problems that go beyond its form. The candidate you vote for is inevitably going to be "right" on some issues and "wrong" on others. Your choice is further confounded by the personal characteristics of the candidates, the incomplete information about them, and the fact that issues and circumstances change after the election so you can't even know when you vote what the issues are going to be.

The Internet created another possible form of democracy: Athenian-style democracy, where the citizenry votes directly on everything. But who could possibly cope with the sheer number and variety of questions that needed to be voted on? And who would even draft the questions or write the laws? Representative democracy in one form or another at least provides a workforce of lawmakers to deal with these enormous tasks.

Another possible form of democracy is the elected dictator. The biggest danger of having an elected dictator is that the dictator, once elected, may suppress the opposition and trample on human rights. Vladimir Putin's rule in Russia is a good example of what can go wrong when a nation is ruled by an elected dictator.

A serious defect of any form of democracy is that it can create a tyranny of the majority. As one of the compromises that led to the ratification of the Constitution, the Bill of Rights was appended to forestall this possibility. The Bill of Rights is profoundly antidemocratic in how it limits the power of the majority.

What Hitler did to the Jews is an extreme example of the tyranny of the majority. Hitler first gained power through a democratic election. He went on to rule Germany as an absolute dictator, but the German people in general supported what he was doing and almost certainly would have reelected him had they been given the opportunity. The imposition of a strict form of Sharia in Algeria by a democratically elected government was thwarted only by forceful intervention by the Algerian military to nullify the election that would have empowered it.

In countries like the United States, regional governments have a great deal of power. Sometimes their political lean is very different from that of the country as a whole. Take the case of Alabama: the city of Mobile almost always votes Democratic but the state of Alabama almost always votes Republican—even when the nation as a whole votes Democratic. "What is the polity?" is a question that confuses the attempt to define democracy.

By what criterion should we judge the success of any form of government? John Stuart Mills's notion of the greatest good for the greatest number was on the right track, but not sufficient since it permits great harm to be done to a small number of people. I have no satisfying answer to that question, but some notion of minimizing harm might come close. In other words, government should do as little harm as possible, and avoiding harm carries more weight than doing good.

What about free speech and other civil rights, or indeed freedom in general? An autocratic government could still be highly responsive to public opinion and allow, indeed encourage, its citizens to express their opinions publicly without fear of reprisal. Nothing in the nature of autocracy precludes that, even if that's not what autocracies usually do. People could be free to advocate for the overthrow of the government as long as they are prevented from actually overthrowing it.

Ultimately, most people judge a government by whether it does the things they want done and doesn't do the things they don't want done. Beyond that, how it derives its power is secondary. My own preference would be to live under the rule of a wise and benevolent dictator, one who did not punish dissent and indeed considered it thoughtfully. Force would be used only as a necessary defense against those who themselves use force.

Essence and Provenance

Does the origin of something really matter?
Wealthy people tend to think so

The essence of a thing consists of its objective properties. The provenance of a thing consists of its history—where it came from and how it came to be. The value of a thing can depend both on its essence and on its provenance, but under what circumstances an individual comes to value provenance over essence reveals much about that person's values.

The term "provenance" is most often used in connection with works of fine art. There is a painting of King Philip IV in the Metropolitan Museum of Art in New York that was supposed to be by the Spanish master Velazquez. In 1973 the museum's curators decided that it wasn't executed by Velazquez himself but instead by an assistant or follower. More recently, however, the museum concluded that it was by Velazquez after all. The essence of the painting remained the same but its provenance, or what its provenance was understood to be, changed. And so, probably, would its price be changed on the art market were it to be offered for sale.

Provenance matters a great deal in the world of fine art and in particular for the market value of artworks. A fake Renoir is not worth much but a real Renoir is—even if the difference can be detected only through chemical tests not available to the ordinary museum-goer. So why does a museum-goer care whether the Renoir is real or fake when the visual appearance of the two is indistinguishable?

On the streets of New York it isn't hard to find vendors hawking Rolex watches at a tremendous discount. Most of those Rolexes, of course, are fakes. What's more, they probably don't work very well and the gold—if it's gold at all—probably wears off after a while. True Rolex watches are valued because of their provenance. Even if you're lucky enough to find a fake Rolex that runs just as well as a real one and whose gold doesn't wear off, it isn't very valuable because it lacks the provenance of a true Rolex. The value of a Rolex lies far more in its provenance than in its essence. But why should the provenance make such a difference?

There are surprisingly many things that are valued more for their provenance than for their essence. Another example is Bayer aspirin. Different brands of aspirin are chemically identical, but for some consumers the Bayer name—or as the ads would have it, genuine Bayer aspirin—still determines the purchase. In groceries, name brands cost more than store brands. According to Consumer Reports, there's no necessary relationship to quality—name brands are sometimes better than store brands and sometimes not. In pharmaceuticals, there is an enormous price difference between proprietary drugs and generic drugs. The pharmaceutical companies invest vast sums of money in trying to convince people that the proprietary drugs are better, but often they are not.

Sometimes, though, provenance may be directly related to essence. That's the argument made for organic or locally produced foodstuffs. If vegetables have been grown without the use of pesticides or chickens have been raised in a free-range environment, they are supposedly both healthier and tastier. Whether that's really the case is unclear. What's certain is that those foodstuffs are costlier. If you believe that the provenance ensures the quality of the essence, then the price premium is worth it. If you don't believe that, then it isn't. There's a good reason why the Whole Foods grocery chain has been nicknamed "Whole Paycheck".

In some cases provenance is all that matters. Take the case of legal documents. If they are not authenticated they are worthless—or more precisely, worth no more than the value of the paper they are printed on. The same goes for historical artifacts. The essence of an Etruscan vase is nothing more than dried clay, and the essence of a letter written by George Washington is only paper. An extreme case of that is paper money, which is ordinarily worthless if it is counterfeit. A top-quality counterfeit bill, however, may actually have some value because it is worth something to those who would pass it off.

Gold coins are an interesting case. If melted down, they may be worth almost as much as their face value, which indicates that they are valued for their essence rather than for their provenance. But looking deeper, we can consider how gold itself derives its value. There's not much you can do with gold—dental fillings or certain uses in electronics, perhaps. But ultimately this is again a case where the value is determined by the provenance, since if gold were as abundant as sand it wouldn't be worth much at all.

Diamonds are also valued because of their scarcity, but even if they were more abundant, they would have value because of their beauty and the costs associated with finding, mining, and cutting them. The issue of provenance became important in the diamond market because of the matter of "blood diamonds"—diamonds mined by rebel groups in Africa whose goal is to destabilize the national government, for purely selfish reasons. The Kimberley Process Certification Scheme is a process set up by the United Nations, designed to certify the origin of rough diamonds from sources which are free of conflict funded by diamond production. The diamond market has endorsed that scheme, with the result that it is quite difficult, though still possible, to sell blood diamonds. In the case of blood diamonds, the provenance actually reduces the value of a diamond to less than what it would be on the basis of its essence.

The stock someone places in provenance seems to be consistent across different areas. Those who value provenance highly in one aspect of their choices will likely value it highly in other aspects of their choices, and wealthy people are often very concerned with it. That is probably because provenance is often seen as a signifier of status, be it the choice of sneaker among teenage males or the choice of couturier among wealthy women. Expensive restaurants often provide elaborate descriptions of the provenance of the ingredients of the items on their menus; for poor people, provenance per se is not usually a consideration in the choice of food.

I usually care much more about essence than provenance. I have no interest in luxury goods and usually prefer generic goods to name-brand ones. Others may feel differently. But according to Consumer Reports, there is no consistent difference in quality between name-brand products and generic ones.

II
Politics & Public Affairs

American Jewry and
the State of Israel

My emotional attachment to Israel conflicts with my disgust at its current government.

I am a secular American Jew. That statement describes my religious identity, my nationality and my ethnicity. And thus I am a member of American Jewry.

I was brought up in a moderately observant household; until my late teens I was loosely kosher. I went to college at MIT, and ironically, it was a remark by the rabbi at the MIT Hillel chapter—a remark I agreed with—that destroyed my belief in God.

What he said was very simple and obvious: either you believe in a God who intervenes in the world or you don't. I could not reconcile the idea of a miracle-performing God with science—particularly physics. And for me, a God who doesn't intervene in Nature is really no God at all. That realization led me to abandon, one by one, every single one of my religious observances. I still won't eat ham, pork, or shellfish, but that's only because I find them distasteful, not because I find eating them in any way sinful.

I have an American-born brother who lives in Israel. His four sons, born in Israel, are dual American-Israeli citizens. Three of them have served in the Israeli Army. Like most American Jews, I have a strong emotional attachment to Israel. When I read news stories about Israelis, I feel a sense of identity with them. These are my people.

But I am repelled by the actions and behavior of the Netanyahu government and its supporters. These include the Haredim, the ultra-Orthodox Jews who have sought, with some success, to impose their beliefs and values on all Israelis. Their prayers are prayers that I myself recited as a child. Those prayers still resonate with me emotionally, even though they no longer have any intellectual value for me. Members of my family still go to shul on the High Holidays, though I won't go near the place.

The Netanyahu government also relies on the settlers, whose treatment of the Palestinians is abhorrent to me. I have no sympathy for Palestinian terrorists, but the Palestinians aren't going away; despite the settler encroachments, they still inhabit most of the West Bank. There are organizations in the United States such as J Street and New Israel that oppose the mistreatment of the Palestinians, and they have sister organizations within Israel.

Most American Jews probably have the same conflicting feelings that I do; they feel the same attachment to Israel even as they deplore its policies. But we must not allow our feelings to be manipulated by the cynical coalition that currently is in power in Israel.

Building Codes Can Solve
the Public Toilet Problem

Unisex restrooms with enough stalls will make the battles over transsexuals in public restrooms go away.

At outdoor events, conflicts about who should be able to use a particular restroom rarely arise; a row of port-a-potties (though often disgusting) averts any such conflicts. In Europe, restrooms are often unisex; they have a row of closed stalls and handwashing facilities. In small shops, there's often just a single bathroom (often for customers only, unfortunately). Again, problem solved.

Interestingly, the Tremont House in Boston, the first major building in America to have indoor plumbing, had a bank of eight water closets on the main-floor hallway, each designed for a single user. The architect felt no need to designate them by gender, because like the outhouses they were based on, they were single-user only.

I haven't yet learned how the practice of having separate men's and ladies' rooms originated, but it set an unfortunate precedent. It clearly involves a double expense, particularly since men's rooms also need stalls. And aside from the "bathroom battles" currently going on, it does not solve the problem of what the father of a a three-year-old girl is supposed to do when the girl has to urinate.

Since the configuration of public restrooms is regulated by municipal building codes, overhauling those codes is the place to start in recognizing the realities of sexual variation. Just as at a state fair, each stall should include both a urinal and a flushing toilet. (As a man, I'm far more comfortable pissing in a urinal than in an open toilet.) Stalls would need floor-to-ceiling partitions, of course, and perhaps some sound insulation. But the overall expense of building a single unisex restroom would almost certainly be less than that of two separate facilities, especially since only one sink (or group of sinks) would be necessary. And of course all of the arguments about transsexuals would vanish.

It will be a difficult transition because of the huge investment in existing facilities, but building codes and the architecture underlying them are the place to start. Builders will surely come up with clever ways to make the transition in existing buildings. The fact that men's and ladies' rooms are usually adjacent makes the necessary construction work much easier.

Some problems will still remain. Athletic facilities, for example, are segregated by gender. But the problems with athletic facilities are subsumed by much larger problems with the rules for gender in sports—such as the permissibility of men who have been surgically transformed into women competing in women's sports. And there are other similar problems in competitive sports, such as the treatment of athletes with artificial limbs that give them an advantage.

The New York Indictments of Donald Trump Are Off the Mark

Donald Trump combines the worst features of a turd and a snake. But the indictments in New York are nevertheless off the mark.

He is certainly guilty of falsifying business records, which is what the charge is. The problem is that he is being charged for each offense with a felony rather than a misdemeanor. For that charge to be a felony, it must be done in support of some other felony. The other felony in this case is violating election law in connection with the 2016 presidential election. He is undoubtedly guilty of that also, but he hasn't actually been indicted for election law violations. Thus the promotion of the charges from misdemeanor to felony is not really justified.

It's just a happenstance that the New York charges ripened before the charges coming out of Atlanta. Fani Willis is an aggressive prosecutor, and her special grand jury has vigorously if unofficially requested an indictment. Why it hasn't been forthcoming is unknown, but I'm sure Ms. Willis has her reasons. The charge of election interference is clear-cut, and if it had come first, the political appearances would have been quite different.

The Perpetual Public Digital Archive

How You Might Preserve Your Digital Legacy

How can we preserve our digital legacies over the long term? I propose the establishment of an enterprise whose mission is that preservation.

There are two separate but compatible reasons to create an enterprise: to bring in money and to provide a service that ought to be available but doesn't yet exist. The enterprise I am proposing would be a nonprofit corporation that would organize and maintain a public digital archive. The archive is designed so that it will endure as long as humanity endures. I was inspired by the perpetual care that many cemeteries offer. Possible models would be the Harvard Board of Overseers or the MIT Corporation.

I call this enterprise "The Perpetual Public Digital Archive", or the Archive for short. Here is the essence of its business plan. The Archive will have a self-perpetuating endowment, managed by a Board of Trustees. When a Trustee leaves the Board either through death or resignation, the surviving Trustees recruit a replacement. A primary responsibility of a Trustee is to ensure the continuity of the Archive by ensuring the continuity of its management.

The price of placing an item in the Archive is is set so as to ensure that the interest will cover the ongoing expenses of the Archive, including of course the salaries of its Trustees. The Archive is feasible—money earns interest and an endowment produces a stream of interest income. That income covers the operating expenses of the Archive and pays the salaries of the Trustees. The salaries of the Trustees should be set to whatever is necessary to motivate them to join the Board and carry out their responsibilities.

The primary purpose of a profit-making organization is to enrich its stockholders. Other purposes might exist, but those purposes are secondary. If a profit-making organization becomes wealthy, its stockholders will and should be receptive to a buyout offer that would end its independent existence. The Archive is organized as a nonprofit for the same reason that hospitals, cemeteries, and universities are usually organized as nonprofits: to ensure its continued existence.

There are certainly existing digital archives such as OneDrive and Dropbox, but these are run by profit-making corporations. The corporations that operate them do not commit to operating them forever. Unlike OneDrive and Dropbox, the only obligations of the Archive are to preserve and make available its contents and to maintain its own existence.

If you believe that your intellectual property has permanent value and want to ensure that it is not lost to posterity, you would do well to preserve it in the Archive. That's how I feel about my essays, how my sister Nan might feel about her poetry, and indeed how many people feel about their creations. Anything capable of being digitized could be preserved in the Archive, including visual images, music, and multimedia artworks.

The service provided by the Archive would be unique; nothing else would compete with it except for another public archive. (There's no reason why there can't be more than one such archive.) The price charged for placing a document in the Archive would be what it costs to put it there, plus what it costs to preserve it, plus the overhead of maintaining the Archive in perpetuity. An initial endowment would be necessary but it could be repaid.

As to the technology, the technologies now used by various organizations to preserve and safeguard their records would suffice over the short term. Over the long term, different technology would undoubtedly be necessary. I don't know what that technology will turn out to be, but the Board would have the responsibility of identifying it and applying it to the Archive.

Trustees would be recruited so as to provide the range of expertise necessary to manage the Archive. Although it would not be a requirement, I would anticipate that a Trustee would want to place some of their own material in the Archive. Trustee compensation would be the fair-market price of services rendered. The Founding Trustee (or Trustees) would formulate the Bylaws of the Archive and recruit the other Trustees. The Founder would necessarily have to believe in the concept of the Archive and have enough entrepreneurial abilities to make it all happen.

The Board of Trustees will have many policy questions to resolve. What should be the rules and procedures for accessing the Archive? Should there be any limitations on what can be placed in the Archive? Should there be a sunset rule on confidentiality? I don't propose to enumerate these issues, much less resolve them; these will be questions for the Trustees to answer.

The Archive would be recorded in a distributed database, but it would still need a location for the primary storage of its records. That location should be someplace both politically and environmentally stable, unlikely to be disrupted by anything short of a meteorite strike. The town of Visp in Switzerland, which I once passed through, struck me as an interesting possibility, though I admittedly don't know very much about it.

The Board of Trustees should be no larger than necessary. The Board members need not all live in the same location. Administering the Archive would probably not be a full-time job once the Archive has been created. If the Archive is to be created, it needs a Founding Trustee. I'm just too old and I just don't have enough energy to take on that responsibility myself, but I'm hoping that by publicizing the idea I can induce someone else to come forward.

The mission of the Archive is complementary to the mission of Medium. Medium's mission is to publish, not to preserve. Being a profit-making enterprise, Medium has no inherent stake in its survival beyond the lifetimes of the people who run it. But the people who write for Medium clearly care about their writing beyond the income it produces. The Archive would enable Medium authors to preserve for posterity the writing they care so much about.

Nuclear Decommissioning: Not Just for Lefties

No one can win a nuclear war.

On the outskirts of Tucson there sits an airfield, the Davis-Monthan boneyard, where military airplanes go to die. Long lines of airplanes rest there, baking in the Arizona sun. These airplanes no longer serve any military purpose; they have been decommissioned. Nuclear weapons deserve the same fate.

Nuclear disarmament encounters a lot of resistance from people who fear that it leaves the nation open to attack without any way of retaliating. Nuclear decommissioning is not the same as nuclear disarmament. Decommissioning leaves our weapons intact; it just imposes a delay before they can be deployed. A decommissioned weapon is in storage—mothballed—and requires time-consuming work to be rendered usable again. Decommissioning provides a "baby blanket" for the fearful.

There is no plausible scenario for usefully deploying a nuclear bomb. It's not enough just to analyze what would happen in a first attack; one must also consider the retaliations that are certain to follow, including ones by allies of the nations involved. Any nation contemplating the use of nuclear weapons has to be able to answer the question "How will it end?".

Our nuclear arsenal can be decommissioned just as those old airplanes have been. No reciprocal action from any other nation is necessary. Indeed, were we to decommission our nukes, other nuclear powers would recognize that the same compelling logic applies to them and follow our lead. At that point, international treaties would be useful in cementing the truce.

The justification for our nuclear arsenal has been that we might need it to respond to a nuclear attack. But an effective response to a nuclear attack need not be nuclear. The United States has spent trillions of dollars on non-nuclear weapons, including submarines, surface naval vessels, aircraft, and missiles with non-nuclear payloads. Any nation that dared attack the United States could be utterly smashed with these weapons alone.

Nuclear weapons are unique. Their pattern of destruction is widespread, roughly circular, and imprecise. It pays no attention to national boundaries. Fallout produces unpredictable effects far from the primary target. Nuclear weapons have no use other than to threaten. For once a nuclear weapon is introduced into a conflict, a cycle of strike and counterstrike is bound to ensue as other nations are drawn into the conflict by their alliances.

The two atomic bombs dropped on Japan achieved their goal of terrifying the Japanese into surrendering, but the circumstances were very specific. Had the Emperor resolved to fight on, his nation would probably have followed him. Had Japan managed to retain significant retaliatory capability, it might have exercised that capability and refused to surrender. The Japanese cabinet was split on the decision to surrender. (Whether we could have subdued Japan without using nuclear weapons and without a land invasion is controversial, though I believe we could.) The usefulness of those atomic bombs, though undeniable, arose from circumstances unlikely to be repeated.

After World War II the United States believed it was threatened by the Soviet Union. Even then, had the Soviet Union launched a devastating nuclear attack on the United States, what would have happened afterwards? It was inconceivable that the Soviet Union could mount a land offensive and come to rule over us. The resources of the United States were spread over too vast a land to be totally conquered by a foreign power based on a different continent. And had the Soviet Union somehow conquered us, it lacked the capability to administer an occupation of our land and our population.

Look at those nations whose budding nuclear capacities have appeared most worrisome: Iran and North Korea. Our government has put enormous energy into the effort to stymie Iran's nuclear development. But suppose Iran did develop nuclear capability, as it is likely to over the long term. What would the Iranians do with it—attack Israel? Israel would retaliate with such overwhelming force that Iran would be destroyed as a functioning nation—no nukes needed. Surely the rulers of Iran understand this.

As to North Korea: Kim Jong-un might well already have the ability to devastate Seattle or be close to acquiring it, but he would never dare use it. As with Iran, such an action would lead to massive retaliation. Kim is capable of devastating Seoul with long-range artillery, so he surely knows we are unlikely to attack him.

Then there's the rivalry between India and Pakistan, both nuclear powers. Over the years there have been ominous incursions from both sides, notably in Kashmir. Yet their nukes have remained grounded because neither side dares use them. The same logic that dictates decommissioning our nuclear arsenal applies to other nuclear powers as well.

Then why not just leave matters as they are? Maintaining a nuclear arsenal carries two major risks even if we are never attacked: accidental launch and acquisition by a non-state actor. Accidental launch can happen if the launch procedures are flawed or if there is a serious international miscalculation. A fanatical group such as Aum Shinrikyo or Al Qaida might obtain a nuclear bomb either by purchasing it from corrupt agents within a power such as Pakistan or by stealing it some other way. Members of such groups are quite willing to give up their lives for their cause and are not deterred by the possibility of retaliation. That's why a nuclear arsenal is dangerous even if it's never intentionally deployed.

The fundamental flaw in the notion that nuclear weapons are useful is the lack of a coherent answer to the question "what happens next?". That question applies whether we're looking at an initial nuclear attack or a nuclear response to an attack. No matter what the follow-on, the aggressor will eventually be worse off than if the attack had never been launched, since the victim or its allies are certain to respond. Japan's helplessness in 1945 will not be repeated.

Hopefully, nuclear weapons will follow the same pattern as biological and chemical weapons. Both can have devastating effects; neither has been deployed on a large scale. That's not just because of the treaties that ban their use, but more because of the recognition by rulers such as Hafez al Assad of Syria that large-scale use would provoke overwhelming retaliation.

Were a nuclear war to get started, global devastation would be inevitable. The rise in radiation levels would gradually kill off all of humanity, a ghastly scenario portrayed in Nevil Shute's 1957 novel "On the Beach". And the last survivors would be asking the question "How did we ever let this happen?".

Nuclear disarmament has been perceived as a leftist cause, and that by itself has created resistance to the idea. Decommissioning rather than disarming would be more palatable. The biggest obstacle to either nuclear disarmament or nuclear decommissioning is that military stockpiles serve domestic political purposes. Powerful economic interests would oppose decommissioning, let alone disarmament, but it's not just that; traditional patriotism and pride in military power would also work against it. The case for nuclear decommissioning must be forcefully made by enlightened people with political power.

The Second Amendment Is a Nullity

A Talmudic analysis of the text and its context

"A well-regulated Militia being essential to the security of a free State, the right of the people to keep and bear Arms shall not be infringed."

That is the literal text of the Second Amendment to the Constitution of the United States. It has been the subject of fierce controversy.

Consider two possible laws:

1. Carrying an assault weapon in public is prohibited.
2. Carrying an assault weapon in public is permissible without restriction.

Two questions can be asked about either of these laws: Is this law constitutional? And is this law wise?

The question of constitutionality and the question of wisdom can and indeed should be separated. In this analysis I consider only constitutionality; my conclusion is that the Second Amendment has nothing to say about it. Indeed, I would argue, the Second Amendment is effectively a nullity that provides no justification for open carry. To support this conclusion, I examine the text of the Amendment in detail.

The Amendment has two parts, separated by a comma: a prefatory (introductory) clause and an operative clause. In this regard it is unique: no other part of the Constitution nor any of its Amendments contains a prefatory clause. The prefatory clause is essential to the interpretation of the Amendment; were it not essential, it would not be there. It is no mere curlicue, and its purpose can only be to explicate how the operative clause is to be interpreted.

Thus, a well-regulated militia is essential; without it, a free State, whatever that is, is not secure, and that would be very bad. Every state is presumed to have a militia, be that the citizenry as a whole or an ad-hoc group of citizens. (The National Guard is an obvious example of a militia.) And the militia must be well-regulated, hence organized and under control; not just any militia will do. An individual is not a militia.

There is some ambiguity as to what a free State is; the capitalization of State is just a stylistic quirk. The Constitution (like Donald Trump!) is inconsistent in its capitalization; it says its purpose is to "ensure domestic Tranquility [and] provide for the common defense." "Tranquility" is capitalized; "defense" is not. It's unclear here whether "State" refers to a state within the Union, the Union as a whole, or some more abstract notion of a state. The difference could affect whether a militia is controlled by a state government or by the Federal government, but it seems pretty well settled that it's the state government.

What is meant by "the people"? In this context it probably means "any citizen".

The case is compelling that only a state militia has a constitutional right to bear arms. That does not, however, preclude a state enacting legislation to grant that right to individuals. Coming back to my two laws, both of them are constitutional. I would argue that allowing open carry is unwise, but that is a different matter.

The Vain Pursuit of Excellence

The Lake Woebegone Fantasy

The humorist Garrison Keillor wrote about Lake Woebegone, an imaginary town in Minnesota where all the children are above average. Such a place, by definition, cannot exist.

The question of who gets admitted to Harvard College is fiercely controversial. Harvard's reputation is enhanced by the fact that it admits only a very limited number of carefully selected students.

Stuyvesant High School in New York City is a public school for the intellectual elite. There have been protests over the fact that the student body is disproportionately Asian and does not include many Colored students. Admission is by competitive exam, so not every student seeking admission is admitted.

But how much of Harvard's storied reputation derives from its uniqueness? Could we have five Harvards, all equally respected, or fifty? The underlying question is whether intellectual excellence should be measured competitively or absolutely.

I believe that it should be measured absolutely, which is how we measure athletic accomplishments such as hiking the Appalachian Trail in a shorter time than anyone else, swimming across the English Channel, or running a mile in under four minutes. In these endeavors, history is the standard.

Assume for the moment that admission to Harvard were to be based solely on SAT scores (with the test recalibrated so that no one could achieve a perfect score). Anyone who scores better than 900, say, is admitted. If more students are admitted than Harvard can accommodate, we build another Harvard. We can extend this model to include any other desirable qualities in a prospective student as long as we can give those qualities a numerical rating.

The Left's Unproductive Focus on Shiny Objects

Racism and abortion access are good causes but the wrong places for the Left to focus its efforts. Eliminating gross economic inequality would be more productive even for these goals.

When you're trying to improve the world, it's vital to be efficient about it. You can't fix everything, so you should focus your efforts on the areas where your efforts will make the most difference.

Consider the issue of abortion access. I'm a firm believer in a woman's right to control her own body, but the main impediments to that right are economic. There are exceptions, to be sure, but a woman who has enough money can almost always arrange a safe abortion if she needs one. It is no coincidence that those who suffer most from the forced closure of abortion clinics are poor and often nonwhite.

Racism, too, is largely an economic problem. While nonwhite middle-class people may still suffer from prejudice, they usually can buy their way around it if they have the money. If, say, you are excluded from a nice neighborhood, you can almost always find an equally nice or even nicer neighborhood as long as you can afford to pay for it.

The focus on racism has a negative consequence: it draws energy and visibility away from the more important task of reducing economic inequality. We see this particularly among college students, where anti-racism crusades are common but crusades to, say, reduce the power of private equity are not to be found.

Being confined to a wheelchair at this point in my life (though until a few years ago I wasn't), I'm particularly attuned to issues of disability access. In many situations, having lots of money won't get me through the door, literally. But disability access isn't a zero-sum game; providing it doesn't generally inconvenience those who don't need it. So although treatment of the disabled might appear to be the same kind of issue as, say, racism, it really isn't.

Resolving the Conflict Between Ukraine and Russia

*The conflict will probably be resolved by a
return to the status before the war*

The conflict between Ukraine and Russia became a bloody and intense war when Russia attacked Ukraine in February 2022 with a sudden invasion, striking at Ukraine's capital Kyiv. Vladimir Putin expected his forces to capture and control Kyiv within days, enabling him to bring Ukraine back under Russian domination. But it was not to be, and the war is still ongoing.

Although neither side will accept it at this point, a reasonable and indeed most likely outcome would be a cease-fire and a return to approximately the situation before the war ("status quo ante bellum"), with Russia retaining control over Crimea and some limited parts of eastern Ukraine—more or less the areas where Russia had de facto control and popular support before the war. The critical components of the agreement would be Ukrainian membership in the European Union, an understanding that Ukraine would not join NATO, and an acceptance of Ukraine's military neutrality and territorial boundaries as permanent. This would give Russia reassurance that it would not be threatened by NATO expansion in Eastern Europe while enabling Ukraine to integrate its economy with that of Western Europe.

This outcome is actually the most likely one, because it returns the region to a state that it was able to tolerate if not delight in before the war. Russia will have to renounce its Greater Russia ambitions, but those ambitions were never achievable. In return, it will gain a greater sense of security. Ukraine will satisfy its desire to be fully part of Western Europe.

The war has killed millions and devastated Ukraine physically, but in those respects it is not unlike the Second World War. Europe recovered from that war and moved far beyond it; Ukraine will do likewise. It will take economic help from the Western nations, but that help is likely to be forthcoming.

The Destructive Power of Ostentation

It is only human to want to show off, but the diversion of wealth into ostentation has become the primary cause of poverty.

Money can buy comfort. With money, you can buy a house with enough land so that you never need be aware of your neighbors. With money, you can have your food prepared for you just the way you like it. If you actually enjoy cooking, you can pay someone to do the tedious preparation of the ingredients and utensils while you do the creative part of putting it all together. With money, you can travel with as much speed, privacy, and convenience as you desire.

Money can also buy provenance, a subject I explored in my essay Essence and Provenance. You can buy a perfectly comfortable and durable pair of running shoes for under $200, or you can spend thousands on a pair of vintage sneakers. You can buy a perfectly accurate Timex watch for under $50, or you can spend over $5 million in a Patek Philippe World timer. You can buy a top-of-the-line Ford Expedition Max for a little under $90,000 or a 2022 Mercedes-AMG One for $2,7 million. Classic cars can go for much, much more.

Yet the cost of comfort is not unbounded. Getting the highest quality of everything without regard to provenance might cost millions of dollars, but not hundreds of millions. For today's titans of private equity, the price of maximum comfort and convenience is just a pittance.

It is ostentation—the desire to show off one's wealth and to outshine other wealthy people—that leads to extreme spending. It is what explains the enormous yachts, huge mansions, large collections of baubles, and extravagant entertainments. It also explains the football stadiums and hospital wings that the ultra-wealthy contribute in return for having their names attached. (Of course, extreme pampering goes along with the naming rights.) Neither comfort nor provenance by itself can account for these acquisitions. Much of the money spent beyond the comfort level is spent on ostentation.

To be sure, not all of it is. The wealthy also spend money on inheritances and donations. But it's clearly possible to tax the rich without impacting their comfort level at all. And we should. Besides, it will let the rich feel virtuous.

In a recent article in *The Atlantic*, Annie Lowrey proposed that we should simply give everyone money. That's an idea I wrote about in 1997, in "A World without Work," which I slightly revised and republished here on Substack. But is the money there to give? The answer is yes. Per capita income in the United States in 2022 was $70,249; globally, it was $10,883. Since most families consist of several people, family incomes are a multiple of that. Per capita wealth in the United States was $259,780; globally, it was $87,489.

These are astounding statistics. The implication is that we can indeed raise large sums by taxing the rich, give everyone money, and still leave the rich very rich indeed—certainly well above the comfort level. I hope it happens.

Joe Biden's Awful Legacy: Clarence Thomas

Joe Biden has been an admirable President, but his botched handling of the 1991 confirmation hearings for Clarence Thomas are the source of many of our troubles.

In a strange way, Joe Biden is responsible for much of the misery in which the country finds itself. I'm not talking about his performance as President, which I find quite creditable. I refer to his actions back in 1991 when he was the Democratic chairman of the Senate Judiciary Committee and the committee was considering the nomination of Clarence Thomas to the Supreme Court. Biden's mishandling of the nomination hearings and the failure of the media to adequately examine Thomas's statements and history led to Thomas being confirmed. That outcome could and should have been averted.

Since ascending to the Court, Thomas has been an essential vote in a number of disastrous decisions. Perhaps the most consequential was in the case of Bush v. Gore, which in 2000 awarded the Presidency to George W. Bush, the son of the President who appointed Thomas.

Famously, Thomas accused his detractors of conducting a "high-tech lynching". Those words were chosen in order to elicit a sympathetic response, so let's look at them closely.

"High-tech" was presumed to mean "on TV", but TV hardly

qualified as high-tech even in 1991. High-tech is usually taken to refer to new technologies, but in1991, TV had been part of most people's lives for over forty years. Lynching involves physically murdering its victim; Thomas was never in the slightest danger of physical violence.

Historically, the victims of lynching were almost all Black, and their race was an essential motive for lynching them. But Thomas's Blackness was not a negative in his nomination. Quite to the contrary, it was a major reason why he was nominated. The Supreme Court vacancy he was to fill was previously held by Thurgood Marshall, a Black man, and the idea of replacing one Black man by another was prominent in his selection. This was the Black seat on the court, and it had to remain that way.

So for Thomas to suggest that he was being attacked for his race turned reality on its head. His race was an essential qualification when George H.W. Bush nominated him, not a handicap. To place a white man in that seat would have been unthinkable.

And what was the worst fate that could have befallen him? That would have been to have his nomination rejected by the Senate, leaving him still sitting in a very comfortable position as a Federal judge—with life tenure in fact. Hardly a fate comparable to dangling from the end of a rope.

So Thomas's use of the phrase "high-tech lynching" must be recognized for what it was—a manipulative and dishonest attempt to cast himself as a victim with a fate that could hardly be more different than a comfortable life as a Federal judge.

So how does Joe Biden enter this story, and for what is Biden responsible? The Senate was under Democratic control at the time, and Biden could have sunk the nomination by calling additional witnesses. Those witnesses would have corroborated Anita Hill's allegation: Clarence Thomas sexually harassed her when he was chair of the Equal Opportunity Employment Commission (a sad irony in itself) and she was working for him. But Joe Biden ended the confirmation hearing without calling those witnesses.

Had those witnesses been heard, their testimony would probably have sunk the nomination. Thomas's presence on the Court was critical to the Republican advance at several moments, notably the 5-4 decision that gave the disputed 2000 election to George W. Bush.

Clarence Thomas's behavior during the hearings gave us the measure of the man. He did not deserve to be seated on the Supreme Court.

Should We Build Homes in Dangerous Places?

The Florida coast and the forests of the Pacific Northwest are desirable but dangerous places to build homes. Is there an economic model that fully reflects that conflict?

The Florida Coast is a very desirable place to live. The high price of beachfront real estate reflects that desirability. The question of whether flood and hurricane insurance for homes built on such properties should be subsidized is vexing and controversial. The situation is similar for homes built at the edges of forests in the Pacific Northwest, for which wildfires are a major risk.

The simplest answer would be to forbid building homes in such places and even to go so far as to demolish those homes that are already there. But to enact such a policy would provoke furious and passionate protest. I believe that a broader perspective is possible.

Would someone want to build a home on the Florida coast with the knowledge that it would be totally destroyed exactly twelve years later? Possibly yes, since a prospective beach dweller would be willing to rent a home for that length of time, knowing that they would have to move out when the rental agreement expired. There is economic value in a home even when it is built in a dangerous place. A rational policy about building, financing, and insuring homes built in dangerous places should recognize but not overstate that value.

The insurance market and the requirements for insurance that apply to homeowners are a sensible way to institute such a policy. But realtors have a strong incentive to oversell the desirability of a property and minimize the risks that go with owning it. To counteract that incentive, strong regulation about how property is marketed and sold is an absolute necessity. Caveat emptor is not good enough.

Insurance requirements must be applied to property no matter how it is acquired. The case of property acquired through gift or inheritance is admittedly tricky. For such property, self-insurance might be permissible. But anyone who self-insures must take full legal responsibility for any damage to the property in question.

The issue of insurance for renters must also be considered. When natural disaster strikes a rental property, the belongings of the renters are also affected. The simplest solution might be to have insurance coverage included as a part of every rental agreement.

The Threat of Nuclear Holocaust

No one can win a nuclear war. Probably no one can even survive one.

Once a nuclear weapon is deployed anywhere, civilization, and likely the human race itself, is doomed. A cycle of attack and counterattack is bound to continue until the world has been made unlivable by worldwide radioactive contamination, with every significant population center destroyed.

Almost every nation in the world is embedded in a web of military and political alliances, so an attack on one nation will draw others into the conflict. Once a nation is struck by a nuclear weapon, the pressure to retaliate becomes irresistible. No government would be willing to leave an attack unavenged.

In considering any possible policy for using a nuclear weapon, the question must always be asked, over and over again, "What happens next?" For each possible action, what are the likely responses? And for each response, what are the likely counter-responses? In other words, "What will end the cycle?" And the inevitable answer is that nothing less than total destruction will end it.

Consider the conflict between Israel and Iran as one of several possible examples. The Israelis have made it clear that if attacked by a nuclear weapon, they will respond in kind. They have deliberately left it ambiguous what other Iranian actions would provoke a nuclear response. It is also unclear under what circumstances a conflict between Israel and Iran might draw in Russia or China—or the United States.

A war between Israel and Iran would be catastrophic, but even more so if it turned nuclear. We cannot expect Israel to simply abandon its nuclear weaponry. But what would be feasible is for Israel to decommission it—to ensure that a considerable national effort would be required to make it serviceable again and therefore to insert a significant delay into any decision to deploy it.

Universal disarmament is not politically feasible. No nuclear power can be expected to withstand the domestic opposition to such a move. But universal decommissioning provides a way around that, enabling a government to say that it still has those weapons in reserve should they be needed. It is, in effect, disarmament lite.

Decommissioning also guards against another danger—rogue agents within a nuclear-armed regime. Part of the decommissioning procedure would be the creation of safeguards against any unofficial reactivation of a weapon. That is a difficult but not impossible challenge,

Another hazard is the existence of rogue groups who don't care if they blow up the world as long as they destroy their enemies. The best defense against such groups is international unity among all nuclear-capable nations.

III
Artificial Intelligence

Customer Service: A Test Case for Artificial Intelligence

Responding to customer service requests is a major expense and a challenge for most large businesses. AI might help, but it's not yet up to the task.

Responding to customer requests for help is a major expense and major challenge for just about any business operating on the Internet. Customers are rarely satisfied with the options they are offered; their most urgent request is usually to talk to a human. Businesses, on the other hand, do their best to dodge and deflect these requests, since providing quality human assistance is enormously, even ruinously, expensive.

This is an example of a benchmark task that tests the capability of artificial intelligence. All of the necessary machinery already exists in some rudimentary form; the difficulty lies in refining and integrating it. It requires speech recognition and synthesis as well as reasoning ability and of course the ability to derive answers from a database.

The first part of the task is understanding the request. The customer may not be speaking distinctly, and even if they are, they may lack the verbal ability to articulate clearly what help they need. Merely clarifying the request may require a dialogue between the agent and the customer.

Then the agent has to explain the answer to the customer, who may have trouble understanding it or performing the actions needed to resolve the issue. The issue may require a complicated conversation between customer and agent. All of this is possible in principle and seems achievable, but the necessary machinery doesn't yet exist.

The criterion for success in attaining this benchmark is simple: the customer feels it would be pointless to speak to a human because the problem has been fully communicated, even though it might not have been resolved. If a complaint is generated, the agent needs to ensure that the complaint is handled by whatever means the agent's owner provides.

Governmental agencies already intercept, monitor, and analyze billions of telephone conversations. The nature and capabilities of the technologies they use are secret, but the fact of their existence suggests that achieving the customer service benchmark is not an unreasonable goal.

When we ask whether we have yet managed to achieve general artificial intelligence, the attainment of benchmarks such as this will go far towards providing an answer.

The Real Danger from
AI Development

Unanticipated side effects of AI development are a real danger. Despite popular fears, spontaneous malevolent agents are not likely to emerge.

In the popular imagination, the world is under threat from alien agents, created by artificial intelligence, taking over the world and turning human beings into slaves. I see that as a very unlikely future. There is just no plausible way for that process to get started, and even if there were, there's no good reason to expect that higher intelligence to wish harm on humanity.

But these fears are a distraction, indeed a redirection, from the thing we need to fear most: unanticipated consequences of benevolent actions. My colleague Seth Schoen has suggested a good example. The roads in the town I live in, Deerfield, Massachusetts, have been badly damaged by heavy flooding, more severe than anything in the town's recorded history. Suppose we were to task an intelligent agent with fixing Deerfield's roads. It might come up with a plan that was far more expensive than anything the town could afford, or a plan that had severe environmental side-effects, or a plan that unfairly exploited an adjacent town. It's impossible to enumerate the specific contingencies that should be avoided. We might say "don't do anything unreasonable", but whether a particular plan is unreasonable is not something an algorithm can determine.

I've been following a series of posts on Medium by Admiral Cloudberg about aviation accidents. They've become very rare, but they still can happen. We haven't abandoned air travel just because we can't exclude the possibility of disastrous crashes.

Similarly, we should approach artificial intelligence with great wariness about the hazards and a determination to identify and avoid them. But the benefits to be derived from artificial intelligence are great, especially the prospect of universal abundance and the global abolition of poverty. The risks can and should be mitigated.

Fact-Checking: A Challenge for Artificial Intelligence

Generative systems by their very nature cannot do fact-checking. Fact-checking is an essential missing piece in the development of artificial intelligence.

Fact-checking is an essential part of journalism. Publications like The New York Times have departments dedicated to it. But agents like ChatGPT are by their nature unable to perform it because fact-checking is not a generative process.

The lack of fact-checking is why chatbots generate nonsense as well as truth. For many applications, this isn't a problem. The nonsense may seem plausible—chatbots are great at producing plausible-sounding text. But that nonsense has led to pervasive pollution in the information environment of the Internet.

I have neither the skills nor the knowledge to be able to create a fact-checker myself, let alone the resources. But having worked in AI and contemplated its powers and limitations for many years, I do feel confident in understanding what the tools of natural language processing can do. There are many researchers who are capable of doing what I am not capable of doing.

The heart of the problem is the representation of knowledge—in other words, facts. Chatbots work with representations of knowledge too. That people are capable of fact-checking is strong evidence that artificially intelligent computers could do it as well. But no one seems to be working on this problem. Some very wise people have written extensively about the limitations as well as the powers of chatbots and the dangers of their widespread use. Yet I have seen no public discussion of using the same tools used to build chatbots in order to build fact-checkers.

I emphasize again that a chatbot is not and cannot be a fact-checker. An airplane is not a submarine, even though similar manufacturing techniques are used to build them. Aerospace engineering and naval architecture are quite distinct disciplines, even though they have common roots.

A related but quite distinct problem is checking mathematical proofs. That was the subject of my doctoral dissertation many years ago, and I reached the negative conclusion that at that time we just didn't have the tools to do it for real mathematics. But my colleague Seth Schoen, who has looked into modern methods of mathematical proof checking, informs me that the state of the art has advanced radically since I worked on it, and we are now near the point where the theorems and proofs published in mathematics journals could be checked by computer. Of course, mathematical facts and facts in the real world are very different sorts of things; fact-checking the one is of no help in fact-checking the other.

Fact-checking is the key missing ingredient in building artificially intelligent agents that we can rely on.

Are We There Yet?

Useful Benchmarks for Artificial Intelligence

Benchmark tasks have been and will be the best way to appraise the success of artificial intelligence.

The term artificial intelligence was coined in 1956 by John McCarthy, then a mathematics professor at Dartmouth College. That year he and Marvin Minsky, a mathematics professor at MIT, jointly organized the Dartmouth Summer Research Conference on Artificial Intelligence. I was Minsky's first doctoral student at MIT, and my doctoral dissertation Machine Verification of Mathematical Proof was based on an idea of McCarthy's. I was introduced to Minsky by Ted Martin, chair of the MIT Mathematics Department, who knew of my interest in computers; Minsky also had an appointment at Harvard at the time, where he was exploring neural nets. A couple of years later he taught the first course on AI to be given at MIT.

The notion that a machine might think goes back much earlier, however. It was contemplated in the 1930s by Alan Turing, who came up with the famous Turing Test as the first and most famous AI benchmark: can a machine conduct a conversation with a human over a communication link in in which that the human cannot tell whether he or she is communicating with a human or with a machine? ChatGPT has convincingly demonstrated that an artificial intelligence can pass the Turing Test.

Another group of benchmarks are based on games. For years, the ability to win the world chess championship was an accepted benchmark; when IBM's Deep Blue defeated Gary Kasparov in 1997, that benchmark was achieved, only to point the way to a more difficult benchmark: the Japanese game of Go. Then the AlphaGo program defeated Lee Sedol, the world Go champion in 2016. So it seems that this class of benchmarks has been exhausted too.

A possible benchmark is in the area of the law. Can an artificial intelligence win cases in court? This is tricky because most court cases require a live human to physically appear as an advocate—but not all do. We can also look at the role of a clerk to a Supreme Court judge. Would a judge find a brief prepared by an intelligent agent such as ChatGPT to be convincing and useful?

Another benchmark might be the resolution of a major unsolved question in mathematics, such as the equivalence or non-equivalence of the computational classes P and NP.

A truly self-driving car is an appealing benchmark, but that benchmark is not well defined. Never getting into accidents is not a workable criterion, since some car accidents are unavoidable. Rationally, the right criterion would be when the safety record of self-driving cars is much better than the safety record of human-driven cars. But the accidents caused by self-driving cars are often quirky and peculiar—things that would never happen with a human at the wheel. That fact mitigates against the acceptance of self-driving cars no matter what the accident statistics are.

I distinguish between benchmarks (like chess) that are purely symbolic and those (like self-driving cars) that require physical apparatus. That apparatus is what robotics provides. ChatGPT and its brethren do amazing things, but they're still tethered to the realm of the symbolic.

So the most radical advances in AI must depend on advances in robotics. My favorite benchmark is the construction of a robot that could clean and make up a hotel room. That task requires physical dexterity, the ability to recognize a wide variety of objects, and significant reasoning ability—quite beyond the powers of anything the robotics industry can build today.

Then there are the sex bots—robots that are supposed to provide people with ecstatically satisfying sexual experiences, like the prostitute in the movie Westworld. But any full discussion of this topic is bound to get caught up subjectivity and in fierce social and political controversy—the more capable the sex bot, the hotter the controversy.

Everyday life is the source of the best benchmarks. I think of what a nurse in a well-run residence for the aged does, or what a plumber does to diagnose and repair a leak. Formulating this kind of work as a set of benchmark tasks is not easy. But having robots that could do these things would revolutionize society.

Could You Ever Love a Robot?

The answer is: it depends

Could you ever love a robot? The answer is actually blindingly obvious: some people could and some people could not. Think of how people relate to cats. Some people (like me) love them and some people hate them. For a cat-hater, no cat can possibly be lovable; even the most adorable kitten is repulsive. If you doubt that, as some ardent cat lovers might, think of snakes. Some people have pet snakes that they love. But like most people, I cannot see myself as ever loving a snake. Some people love their cars. Some people love their robotic toys.

The qualities of any creature can be classified as inherent or performative. Its inherent qualities are what it is; its performative qualities are what it does or is capable of doing. I don't see a clear upper bound on the performative qualities of robots; I'm agnostic as to whether such a clear upper bound exists. The way people react to cats or robots is based more on the inherent qualities of robots than on the performative qualities of robots.

The Star Trek video series featured a number of robots with human qualities. You can think of those videos as an exploration, in part, of the lovability of robots.

Missing from the Chatbots: Critical Ability

Chatbots lack an understanding of truth as relative.

Artificial intelligence will take a big step forward when it can handle the notion of falsity—when it can understand that not all statements it finds are true. This is a very difficult and hard-to-specify task, given that truth is, in the real world, determined by a social process. I examined this process in my essay How We Know What We Know here on Substack. Even mathematical proof, considered to be the highest standard for truth, has occasionally been shown to be faulty (see, for example, this accounting of correct results with incorrect proofs).

Yet the need to determine truth, at least pragmatically, is unavoidable. That's what court trials are all about. We recognize different standards of truth—"preponderance of evidence", "beyond reasonable doubt"—because we have to. We have websites such as Snopes and Politifacts devoted to evaluating the truth of public statements found on the Web and elsewhere.

Given what has already been achieved by generative AI, I believe this capability is achievable, but we need to understand what that achievement means. A judgement by an intelligent agent should always be understood as ultimately contingent, even if for practical purposes we have to treat it as absolute. It's much like the situation with the safety of self-driving cars. We can't reasonably expect them to be perfectly safe; the most we can strive for is for them to be much safer than cars driven by people. The accidents that befall self-driving cars are often peculiar and surprising, but that by itself does not make such cars any less safe.

I believe but cannot prove that as the technology gets better, machines will be able to make more accurate and acceptable judgements than people. The test will come if and when we start using them in courtrooms. Will their decisions be accepted? As with self-driving cars, we'll see when we start deploying them.

What Chatbots Don't Do

Chatbots predict utterances. They don't attempt to decide if an utterance is true or false.

A group of engineers decide to build a tower to the moon. Every month they proudly announce how much taller the tower is. The trouble is that the moon isn't getting any closer.

Thus it is with chatbots and general artificial intelligence. Chatbots don't recognize the existence of an external world in which some statements are true and, most importantly, other statements are false. Lacking that recognition, they can't get there from here.

The essence of the scientific method is that you formulate a hypothesis and determine its truth through experiments. Chatbots don't do that. They are in the business of generating predictions; once they have generated a prediction, they have no way of declaring it incorrect later on. That's why we haven't seen chatbots that do the sort of fact-checking that websites like Snopes and Politifacts do.

Programs like Alpha Go are different from chatbots. Their behavior is subject to an external discipline: do they win the game or do they lose it? It's not just that winning formulas are found; losing strategies must be deselected. That behavior needs to be married to the chatbots.

I await the creation of an intelligent agent that formulates hypotheses about the external world and then goes about testing them. Children do this; even animals do this. I believe that computers can do this too. But so far, they don't.

IV
A Signature Piece

The World Without Work

*Can we have a world where machines do all the work?
And would we want it?*

This essay appeared in the book Beyond Calculation, *a collection of invited papers published in 1996, the fiftieth anniversary of the founding of ACM, on the theme of "The Next Fifty Years of Computing." It was edited by Peter Denning and Bob Metcalfe and published by Copernicus, an imprint of Springer-Verlag. It has quite a few obvious anachronisms; nevertheless, much of it is still meaningful today. I have chosen to retain those anachronisms rather than update them.*

Imagine a world where smart machines do all the work—a world in which man no longer lives by the sweat of his brow. Intelligent robots, freely available to all, provide all the economic benefits of slavery without any of its moral and ethical drawbacks. Want a new home? Just ask a robotic architect to design your dream house, a crew of construction robots to build it. Want to travel to a faraway place? A robot taxi can take you to the airport, where a robotically piloted aircraft can whisk you to your destination. Ready for dinner? A few words to your robotic chef and the food will be prepared just as you wish, with inventive touches ensuring that no meal is exactly like a previous one—unless you want it that way, of course.

Looking for diversion? An authorial robot can create a new, unique entertainment for you in any medium, be it a simulated football game, a rock video, a baroque cantata, or an oil painting. Want to play tennis or chess? A perfectly matched robotic opponent awaits you.

Are you physically ill? A robotic physician, possessing all the medical knowledge known to civilization and the dexterity of the perfect surgeon, will see to your cure. And despite your life of comfort and luxury, are you sick at heart? Talk as long as you wish with a robotic therapist—ever patient, never judgmental, always wise and insightful.

I was a graduate student at MIT in the late 1950s and early 1960s when the field of artificial intelligence, fathered by my advisor, Marvin Minsky, was just getting started. In those heady times, machines that could think seemed to be no more than a couple of decades away. The General Problem Solver program of Newell, Simon, and Shaw appeared to offer deep insight into how the human mind worked and the prospect of being able to simulate it on a computer. Their paper on the General Problem Solver Self-Applied proposed an exciting model of how computers could program themselves to be intelligent. The model ran into a few programming difficulties, but we all thought that those difficulties would not be hard to overcome. Experience showed otherwise: the General Problem Solver Self-Applied was never successfully implemented.

In the hubris of those days, I thought a lot about what people would do when intelligent machines did all the work. I imagined the computer of the future as an intelligent, capable slave, offering the promise of the benefits of slavery without any of its moral and ethical drawbacks. I contemplated how people would spend their time in the "world without work" and how people would respond to computer-created art or how well they could be helped by computerized psychiatrists.

More than thirty years later, despite extraordinary progress in computer technology, the promises of artificial intelligence remain unfulfilled. It's as though a group of people had proposed to build a tower to the moon. Each year they point with pride at how much higher the tower is than it was the previous year. The trouble is that the moon isn't getting much closer.

Hubris about what computers can do has been with us since the early days of computing. About the time that ACM was created fifty years ago, one of its founders, Edmund Berkeley, was publishing the magazine Computers and Automation, which often described "giant brains" in glowing terms. We can see the same kind of hubris today in the bright portraits of the Information Superhighway painted by publications such as Wired magazine. To be sure, other fields of science and technology share that hubris—think of the world of nearly free electricity that nuclear power was once supposed to bring us via the Atoms for Peace program or the ambitious plans for space exploration that captured the imagination of Americans in the Sixties.

An instructive example of the unfulfilled promises of artificial intelligence is the fate of the Fifth Generation Computer Project, sponsored by the Japanese Ministry of International Trade and Industry in the 1980s. Edward Feigenbaum (himself an AI pioneer) and Pamela McCorduck described it in their book *The Fifth Generation: Artificial Intelligence and Japan's Computer Challenge to the World*. In 1983 they wrote:

> *The vehicles of revolution are to be known as knowledge information processing systems. . . . The Japanese expect these new computers, which users will be able to speak with in everyday conversational language . . . to penetrate every level of society. . . .They will not even require the user to be very specific about his needs, because they will have reasoning power and will be able to tease out from the user, by questioning and by suggestions, just exactly what it is the user wants to do or know. . . . The Japanese expect these computers to be the core computers— that is, the computers most generally in use worldwide—by the 1990s.*

Although the Fifth Generation Project may have accomplished a great deal, these 1983 predictions (by Americans, it must be said, not the Japanese) have little connection to where we are in 1996.

The world without work seemed both plausible and appealing when I contemplated it in my graduate student days. Now, several decades later, I've come to reexamine that world. Is it technically feasible? Assuming it's technically feasible, can society make the transition to a world without work? What are the limits in principle to what machines can do in the world without work? And how much better is a world without work than the world we live in now?

The prospects aren't very bright that we'll soon be able to build the marvelous robots that make the world without work possible. Most of the amenities of the world without work require not just raw artificial intelligence but also robotics—using sensors and actuators so that the computer could analyze and act on its environment. Simulating the behavior of human sensory organs is a particularly difficult task for computers, at least given what we know so far about how to do it.

Not all the work to be done in a robot-served world requires sensory input. Some tasks only require the computer to analyze and react to data presented in textual form. Yet even these tasks are often far beyond what current software can do. For instance, there are many programs now on the market that check text for errors in spelling, grammar, and usage, but these programs do a pitiful job indeed compared with what a human proofreader does.

A good example of a difficult task for computers is the task of answering the telephone at a large company. Switchboard operators at those companies have largely been replaced by automated response systems, which callers almost invariably dislike. But imagine a computer that could do what a human operator does: interpret what a caller is saying (and not just by limiting the caller to a restricted vocabulary), ask whatever questions are necessary; and either answer the caller's question or dispatch the call to the appropriate person.

This task, which is not difficult for a human being with a modicum of intelligence, calls for freeform speech recognition and interpretation as well as a lot of commonsense reasoning. These capabilities are well beyond the state of the art in artificial intelligence.

Here's another example: building a robotic taxi for New York City that can understand the passenger's instructions and carry the passenger safely to the destination. Among other things, this task calls for real-time visual analysis of complex street scenes, understanding freeform speech from many speakers (as in the switchboard example), and a good deal of rather complex reasoning about the best way to get from one place to another under widely varying traffic, obstructions, and other conditions. And to really perform this task with style, the taxi-robot would have to be able to entertain the passenger with jokes when it gets stuck in traffic.

Coming back to tasks that don't require sensory input, consider what it would take to produce a faithful translation of a literary work into a foreign language. A word-for-word translation will hardly do. The computer needs to understand both languages, of course. But more than that, it needs to understand what the book is about. It needs to capture and translate the author's style, understanding the allusions, idioms, and metaphors in a way that is true to their intent. And it needs to perceive and preserve the multiple levels of meaning inherent in the text. Providing such a deep understanding of natural language, even in its written form, is far beyond anything we know how to do today.

In my idealized portrait of the world without work, I brought up the notion of a robotic chef. Collecting recipes and measuring ingredients would be easy enough—but how about tasting the ragout to correct the seasoning? There's a long way to go from chemical analyses to a simulation of our senses of taste and smell, and a long way from a simple simulation of those senses to a program that could capture the aesthetics of cuisine.

Then there are all the low-paid, physically or psychologically stressful jobs that so many people perform out of necessity: fruit and vegetable harvesting, garment manufacturing, carpet weaving, cleaning and janitorial work, service, and so forth. These jobs have resisted full automation because they call for complex pattern recognition and flexibility, even though they can be performed by people with no formal education.

It's one thing to design a robot that can navigate around a room without bumping into things, quite another to design a robot that can harvest the fruit from an apple orchard. Picking an apple requires locating the apple within the surrounding leaves and branches, assessing its ripeness, maneuvering around obstacles to grasp it without bruising it, and detaching it from the tree with just the right amount of force. These are easy tasks for a person, very difficult ones for today's computers.

In a remarkable irony, computerization itself has created a major automation-resistant job: data entry. Computerized databases have a voracious appetite for information, and it takes an army of typists at computer screens to feed them. While some printed information can be processed using optical scanners, human beings still have to check the results for accuracy and correct the inevitable errors.

It will be hard enough to create smart machines that can perform tasks like these. But that won't suffice for tasks where the machine must interact with people. If machines are to serve us well, they have to perform those tasks in a human-sensitive way. In his book *Things That Make Us Smart*, the cognitive scientist Donald Norman notes how often computer-based systems force people to conform to the attributes of the machine and therefore don't work very well.

Automated-response telephone systems are a good example. These computer-based systems may save money for the companies that use them, but only by shifting work to the callers. To make matters worse, their design is often user-hostile. They compel you to listen to a sequence of alternatives before you get to the one you want—if it's there at all. And if you don't realize which alternative you need until you've heard the entire list, you have to go back and listen to it all over again. It's no wonder that people almost always prefer to talk to a human being.

There's yet another technological problem in building the machines of the world without work. It's not enough to make our machines work; we have to make them work reliably, or at least control what happens when they don't work as they're supposed to. We've learned from sad experience that computer systems have failure modes as novel as computers themselves were when they were first built, and that the consequences of computer failures are often strange, unexpected, and far-reaching. The more we invent, the more failure modes we discover. Reliability engineering is an important subdiscipline of software engineering, but its record of success is spotty at best. A solid theory of how to build reliable systems continues to elude us.

For many years the noted software engineer Peter Neumann has been running a Risks Forum, reporting on the failures of various partially or fully automated systems and their consequences to the public. Less than a year after California's Pelican Bay State Prison was opened, the inmates figured out how to pop open the supposedly escape-proof pneumatic cell doors. The San Francisco Muni Metro was long plagued by a ghosting problem in which the signaling system insisted that a nonexistent train was blocking a switch. A Northwest Airlines DC-9 crashed over Detroit in 1987 because the flaps and the thrust computer indicator had not been set properly before takeoff.

All kinds of engineering artifacts have failure modes, not just computers. Computer scientists often cite civil engineering as an example of a discipline that knows how to build reliable structures, yet bridges and buildings do collapse now and then. The failures of computer systems have a particularly exotic quality to them, however; computer systems rarely fail in mundane ways. Murphy's Law—that almost anything that can fail will fail—bedevils nearly every effort we make to better our lives by modifying our environment, and not only when it comes to computer-related technology. The gypsy moth caterpillar, once thought to be a superior silkworm, escapes confinement and ravages the deciduous trees of the northeastern United States. The zebra mussel escapes from the ballast water of oceangoing ships and clogs intake pipes throughout the Great Lakes region. Chlorofluorocarbons chew holes in the ozone layer. Miracle pharmaceuticals lead to new mutations of viruses and microbes, creating ever more drug-resistant infections. If we can't prevent the side effects of our wondrous machines from causing these sorts of disasters, those machines will not have bettered our lives.

So technological challenges exist on several levels. First, there are specific tasks that computer technology, and artificial intelligence in particular, is far from mastering. Next is the challenge of getting machines to behave in a human-sensitive way, well beyond the current art of user-interface design. After that, we must deal in a systematic way with the problem of unreliability and its sometimes catastrophic consequences.

One tempting response to these challenges is that we might eventually be able to build computer programs in the spirit of the General Problem Solver Self-Applied—programs that not only design the technologies we need but also figure out how to deal with whatever unfavorable consequences those technologies might bring. That kind of symbolic task is actually easier for computers than tasks where they have to sense and manipulate their physical environment directly. However, the thought of such powerful thinking machines raises the scary issue of whether we would have enough foresight to control their path of development. Were we to fail in that, we could well find our lives controlled by machines in ways we never intended.

None of these challenges are anywhere near to being met, and the prospect that all of them will be met within the next half century is slight indeed. A technological optimist would say that it's just a matter of time; a technological pessimist would doubt it. History may be full of pessimists who were proven wrong, but lots of optimists have been proven wrong when they were foolhardy enough to attach dates to their predictions. The optimists may argue that if something hasn't yet happened, we only have to wait a while longer. But will we have to wait forever?

There's a story about a traveler in Vermont who lost his way while driving through the countryside. Seeing a grizzled old farmer working near the side of the road, he stopped to ask directions to Rutland. "Rutland, eh?" said the farmer. "Oh, you can't get there from here." Let's assume that the technological optimists are right—that within the next half century, we will indeed invent the smart machines that will finally enable artificial intelligence to fulfill its extravagant promises. We then run up against the second difficulty with the world where no one has to work: can we really get there from here, given the obstacles our economy and culture places in the way of the transition?

In a recent article in the New York Times Magazine, the economics writer Peter Passell asked the question. Why doesn't the best always win? Why doesn't the best technology survive the rough-and-tumble of the free market? In answer, he described the phenomenon of path dependence—the way that small, random events at critical moments can determine whether or not a useful or superior technology is actually deployed. Once those events have occurred, their outcome is extremely difficult and expensive to change.

The classic example of path dependence is the QWERTY typewriter keyboard, so named because QWERTY is the sequence of keys on the left side of the top row. This example was examined by Paul David, an economic historian at Stanford, in a 1985 article called "Clio and the Economics of QWERTY" Originally designed to prevent early mechanical typewriters from jamming when common sequences of keys were struck too rapidly in succession, the QWERTY keyboard became effectively locked in. People use it because it is universally available and standardized; it is universally available because people demand it. Other keyboard layouts that enable people to type more rapidly and less stressfully have been designed, most notably the Dvorak keyboard, but they've made little headway against QWERTY. The force of the standards and practices of a very large community is simply too powerful to overcome.

Another of Passell's examples is the adoption of Matsushita's VHS standard for videocassette recorders over Sony's technically superior Betamax system. The original Betamax machines were limited to one-hour tapes, too short to play an entire movie. Although this was not a fundamental limitation—Sony could have produced longer tapes but was rushing to get the product out the door—it provided the market opening that Matsushita was able to exploit. The Betamax system was never able to overcome the rapid penetration of VHS into the marketplace.

Although path dependence has been thought of mainly in terms of its effects on the adaptation of specific technologies, it also describes quite well the way the work ethic would make it very difficult for a society such as ours to adapt to and accept the world without work. The work ethic is deeply embedded in nearly all Western societies and appears in various forms in other societies as well. It has two aspects: first, the belief that work is virtuous and godly; second, the insistence that those who are able to work ought to work.

We probably could design an economic system in which the existence of free, plentiful, and intelligent labor would be turned to the advantage of all. But it almost certainly would have to be a system in which people were neither expected nor asked to work for a living, since there simply would not be enough useful, let alone necessary, work to go around. And for a society that believes in the work ethic, such a system would be very hard for most people to accept.

To understand this obstacle to achieving the world without work, think about how difficult it is for a highly developed nation to utilize cheap overseas or immigrant labor without severe damage to its social fabric. Businesses, of course, have historically used overseas or immigrant labor to lower their costs and often (but not always) have passed on the savings to consumers. You'd think that cheap labor would obviously be beneficial to society because it makes goods and services easier to obtain (the moral issues created by the laborers' working conditions aside). But since cheap labor by foreigners usually depresses the wages of native workers and often abolishes their jobs altogether, native workers have fought it fiercely. This struggle has taken place not just in the United States but in several European countries, notably France and Germany, as well.

Smart machines are, of course, the ultimate form of cheap labor, and the harshness of their working conditions is not a moral issue. But workers respond to automation much as they do to competition from cheap labor. Adam Smith once pointed out that candlemakers are in competition with the Sun, and that a world of darkness would improve their prospects enormously. Most workers respond like Adam Smith's candlemakers to the thought of their jobs being automated out of existence, even if the net economic effect of automation might be beneficial (for example, creating new jobs for a different class of workers). And without the total restructuring of society that abandoning the work ethic would imply, who could blame them?

So even if we could solve all the technological problems of constructing smart machines that would do nearly all of humankind's work, we would still have to face the problem of how to introduce those machines into our socioeconomic systems without ripping apart the fabric of our society. It isn't enough to plan a world in which the work ethic no longer governs our social structures; we need a way to get there. And getting there would be far more difficult than getting to a world in which keyboards followed the Dvorak layout and video- cassette recorders followed the Betamax standard. The work ethic is likely to prove to be the QWERTY keyboard of the world of smart machines.

But suppose, despite all these difficulties, we could build truly smart machines and create the technology to support the world without work. Suppose in addition that we could somehow overcome or bypass the obstacles the work ethic poses to the effective and universal deployment of our smart machines. Daunting as these technical and societal obstacles are, I know of no convincing argument in principle that says they can never be overcome. But having overcome them, we would still have to face the most fundamental difficulties with that idealized world in which no one need work and all can prosper: the limits in principle of what smart machines—robots, that is—can do. These limits dictate the answers to the two questions that matter the most: to what extent can robots replace people? And can robots make the world a much better place in which to live?

No matter what we can achieve technically, there will always be a distinction between machines and people. That distinction is a critical one because so much of our response to other creatures, be they humans, animals, or machines, is deeply rooted in our instincts. We respond to people in a certain way precisely because they are people. A machine could never meet those human needs where humanness matters.

It's doubtful, for instance, that you could ever feel the same kind of love for a robot you can feel for a person, or even the same quality of sexual attraction. Bisexuals aside, it's somewhat unusual for a heterosexual to be sexually attracted to a member of the same gender or a homosexual to a member of the opposite gender. If most people of the "wrong" gender cannot tap into our libidos, it's unlikely a robot ever could. True, people can be sexually aroused by photographs and drawings—but beneath that arousal lies the knowledge that there's at least an imaginary human being behind the picture.

And when people become aroused by what's often called cybersex, they are well aware that there's usually a real person at the other end of the conversation.

In a similar vein, it's hard to see how a machine could inspire or lead. Leadership and charisma are inherently human qualities. We respond to a Winston Churchill or a Mother Theresa not only because of what that person says and does, but because of who that person is. Leadership is rooted in courage, and courage is meaningful only for a creature that cares about its own survival in a way no computer ever could. And though I can imagine a computer preaching a sermon, I can't imagine the congregation shouting "Amen, brother" in response.

The thought of a robotic psychiatrist raises some related questions. According to orthodox Freudian and other psychoanalytic theory, an essential part of the analytic process is transference and countertransference—basically, the subconscious projection of feelings by the patient onto the therapist or vice versa. What sort of transference is possible when the therapist is not a human being? What does the notion of countertransference even mean for a robotic psychiatrist that has no subconscious and no way of "listening with the third ear"? And does the lack of transference and countertransference seriously compromise the possibility of effective therapy (assuming, of course, that these phenomena are as essential as the Freudians assume they are)?

How we respond to people affects how we respond to the artifacts they produce. Take art, for example. We respond to it not only because of its physical manifestation but also because of its provenance. What's on the canvas isn't all that matters; we also care who painted it, how, and why. Otherwise, why would we value originals over forgeries? A skillful forgery may appear to be just as beautiful as the original, but we value it far less or not at all once its origin has been exposed. Were a computer to produce magnificent sculptures as judged by the usual criteria of the fine arts, we might find those sculptures interesting—but our emotional, intuitive response to them would inevitably be muted by their lack of human provenance.

Some of those most skeptical of using computers to replace people are themselves computer experts. Clifford Stoll, an astronomer and authority on computer security, is one of them. In his book *Silicon Snake Oil*, Stoll questions the nature of the interaction between people and computers. He observes that computers substitute mediated experience for direct experience and points out what is lost in the transition. "No computer can convey what a walk through a pine forest feels like", says Stoll. "Sensation has no substitute".

Stoll catalogues a variety of computer-human interactions in which mediated experience is replacing immediate experience, leaving us worse off. Face-to-face conversation gives way to "net chat". Computer-based instruction replaces the inspiring teacher. Online library catalogs replace helpful librarians. A human quality is lost, and even the cleverest and best-designed of computer systems cannot replace it.

As these examples show, some of the qualities that make people irreplaceable have little to do with how cleverly we can program our computers—or even how cleverly they can program themselves. Making smart machines more humanoid won't change this. After all, how human-like could a robot ever be? Would it eat? Bleed? Die? Procreate? Take pleasure or feel sorrow? If, through some almost unimaginable miracle of technology, we somehow managed to build humanoid robots, would we feel that those creatures were truly human? Would we consider them to be subject to the same moral imperatives as are the children of humans? Could we without compunction treat them as slaves? And if not, then what, other than intellectual curiosity or a desire for power, would be the point of building them—since humans can create other humans easily (and pleasurably) enough?

If we think of the world without work more narrowly, attempting only to free ourselves from tasks where the humanness of the worker isn't essential, the world without work becomes possible in principle at least. And we're probably better off that way; though the necessities of life would be free in such a world, the luxuries—namely, those services that only humans could render—would not be. You could get a machine to rub your back tirelessly for hours on end—but if you wanted a massage from a person, you'd have to pay for it.

I now turn to the other basic question: Can smart machines make the world a much better place to live? In particular, how much can smart machines do to put an end to human misery? When you're selling hammers, all the world's a nail. All too often, people who tout technology talk about what the technology can achieve without much reference to what for most people is actually most critical to leading a happy and satisfying life. Take, for instance, the recent enthusiasm for the World Wide Web. The Web provides novel and powerful ways to retrieve information—but retrieving the kinds of information available over the Web, or any information at all for that matter, plays a limited part in most people's lives. Indeed, the Web offers not the slightest benefit to the majority of the earth's population. It's not merely a coincidence that a typical portrayal of the wonders of the Web invokes as its example a high-school research project— preferably one involving either dolphins or Shakespeare. These examples, that often appear in books and articles on how to use the Web, create a warm and fuzzy image for certain middle-and upper-class populations, but they're utterly irrelevant to most of humanity.

When we look at the sources of human misery, conflict ranks high among them. It may take the form of an interpersonal vendetta or an intense ethnic feud enduring for centuries. Many conflicts have their roots in poverty, something that computers might help us overcome, but not all conflicts do. The families of millionaires are beset by quarrels and hatred; rich nations still wage war on each other. The bitterness between Hindu and Muslim, Serb and Croat,

Arab and Jew, or Hutu and Tutsi often is rooted in a struggle over ancestral land, a struggle in which one side or the other is bound to lose because both sides can't exclusively own and occupy the same land simultaneously. These conflicts are zero-sum games; no machine intelligence or computer-induced abundance can resolve them amicably.

Nor are computers of much help in resolving the moral controversies that stem from different views of how we ought to lead our lives. For those who view homosexuality as an utter abomination, no amount of earthly riches nor any rational argument can persuade them to tolerate it. Those devout Muslims who viewed the writer Salman Rushdie as a blasphemer deserving to be put to death could not be reconciled with those who believed in untrammeled literary expression. Supporters of reproductive freedom for women battle those who believe in the absolute sanctity and personhood of the fetus. Technology stands powerless in the face of these bitter disputes that make lives miserable when people act on their beliefs.

There's another aspect of the world without work that would disturb some people: it would take a powerful, socialistic government to support it and make it possible. Someone or something has to ensure that all those free goods are manufactured and distributed and all those free services are provided. Yet this government could well accommodate a degree of personal freedom we're not accustomed to, since it would not need to regulate individual behavior in order to perform its functions. There's much irony in that, since socialism and individual freedom are considered by some to be incompatible values. To be sure, the regents might be computers rather than people, but that's not necessarily an improvement.

There also remains the question of whether people could lead satisfying lives in a world without work. Retired people on generous pensions sometimes find themselves at loose ends, not knowing what to do with their time. Many wealthy people work tirelessly even though they could afford not to. Is it just work ethic in effect here, or do people have some more fundamental, instinctual need to feel that they're productive members of society?

The world without work, if we could ever achieve it, would be a better place to live. Even partial progress towards that world would be beneficial. Machines (not just computers) have made our lives easier and have immensely amplified our physical and mental abilities. That in itself is an enormous contribution to human welfare. And to the extent that we can substitute computational effort for the consumption of natural resources, computers can help solve an array of environmental problems.

The earth's resources and carrying capacity are finite, but through the clever use of computers we may be able to stretch them. For example, smart machines might enable us to exploit low-grade ores that are not now economical to mine and to scrupulously repair the earth after the ores have been extracted. They might be able to sort trash so that we could recycle almost all of it with no human effort at all.

There's also the tantalizing prospect that smart machines might someday be able to advise us on how to improve our lives and our society—and also know how to get us to take their advice. It may be that humans just aren't smart enough to figure out how to deal effectively with their own problems. If computers can ever do that for us through advances in artificial intelligence, they will truly have become the most beneficial artifacts humanity has ever conceived.

Afterword

Turning Paul's essays into a book has been a gift for both of us. He is my oldest brother by eight years. I was nine years old when Paul went off to M.I.T. It has only been in our adult lives that we've shared experiences of biking and hiking together; and two memorable decades of Thanksgiving family gatherings at his home in Deerfield. Paul has also been a wonderful advisor and loving brother. So what better way to reciprocate than to collaborate on this book and have it serve as his intellectual legacy on the occasion of his 89th birthday.

Nan Rubin
Author's sister

About the Author

Paul Abrahams was born in 1935 in Brooklyn, New York, and grew up in the Five Towns community on Long Island. As an undergraduate he studied mathematics at MIT, graduating in 1956. Continuing on to graduate school at MIT, he became the first student of Marvin Minsky, wo created the field of artificial intelligence. His doctoral dissertation, *Machine Verification of Mathematical Proof*, was jointly supervised by Minsky and John McCarthy

He was a professor of computer science at New York University from 1968 to 1980. While at NYU, he became very interested in the PL/I programming language. An amalgam of FORTRAN, COBOL, and Algol 60, PL/I was the most ambitious programming language of its time. Taking it as a challenge to implement it, he developed CIMS PL/I on NYU's Control Data 6600 computer. That implementation was a tour de force of computer programming.

He became a member of Committee X3J1 of the American National Standards Institute, which developed a national and international standard for PL/I, and played an important role in formulating that standard. He has lectured and written widely about

Standard PL/I and about the definition of programming languages more generally.

He was elected chairman of the ACM Special Interest Group on Programming Languages (SIGPLAN) in 1979. That position led to him eventually becoming President of ACM, the leading professional society in computing, from 1986 until 1988. He is the author of two books: *TeX for the Impatient* and *Unix for the Impatient*.

Computing has hardly been his only interest. He is a devoted and knowledgeable lover of classical music, particularly that of the Baroque period. In 1976, while on sabbatical leave from NYU, he built a two-manual harpsichord from a Zuckerman kit; that instrument is now in use at the Greenwood Presbyterian Church in Warwick, Rhode Island. He also played the oboe for a number of years.

An enthusiastic mycophile, he delighted in collecting and cooking wild mushrooms, both from places near his home and on his travels. He was a regular participant in the Northeast Mycological Foray and in the North American Mycological Association Annul Foray. But he heeded the adage that "there are old mushroomers and bold mushroomers, but there are very few old bold mushroomers".

He lives in Deerfield with his wife Eva, who is an artist and expert builder. She also operates a studio for the creation of electronic music. His beloved daughter, Jodi, is the mother of his three young grandchildren: Nitzan, Adva, and Ziv.

Copies of this book can be purchased on
Amazon.com
and other online bookstores